The Mill Is Burning

The Mill Is Burning

Poems

RICHARD MATTHEWS

Grove Press
New York

Published simultaneously in Canada
Printed in the United States of America

FIRST EDITION

Library of Congress Cataloging-in-Publication Data

Matthews, Richard (Richard J.)
     The mill is burning / Richard Matthews.—1st ed.
       p. cm.
     ISBN 0-8021-3886-1
     I. Title.
     PS3613.A85 M55 2002
     813'.54—dc21   2002017506

DESIGN BY LAURA HAMMOND HOUGH

Grove Press
841 Broadway
New York, NY 10003

02   03   04   05   10 9 8 7 6 5 4 3 2 1

for the lost,
my parents,
Clare Hogben Matthews (1925–1999)
and
James Matthews (1930–1982),
and the found,
my beloved
Joanne

Contents

Acknowledgments

I am grateful to the editors of the following publications in which some of the poems have appeared: *Drunken Boat, The Paris Review, Western Humanities Review,* and *PEN America.*

My thanks for contributing so much to this book to all my wonderful teachers and colleagues, especially April Bernard, Lucie Brock-Broido, Alfred Corn, Monica Ferrell, Jennifer Gossetti, Patrick Masterson, Ryan Murphy, Marie Ponsot, Alice Quinn, Margaret Ryan, Michael Scammell, Nancy Schoenberger, Ravi Shankar, Paul Stephens, and most especially, Nicholas Christopher, whose kind and enduring advocacy made so much possible. Thanks to family, Michael, Paul, Frances, Deborah, Marjorie, Gary, Kelly, Holly, Emily, Thomas, and Pam, for their support and for keeping faith; to Rob Cassella for a place to work; to PEN/America and Alexander Kaplen for their generosity; to Michael Werner Gallery and Georg Baselitz for kind permission to use the cover painting; to Joan Bingham, Zelimir Galjanic, Hillery Stone, Charles Woods, and Michael Hornburg at Grove Press for making this book possible and for making the process of producing it an education and a pleasure.

My greatest gratitude, love and admiration (which will always seem teaspoons wielded at the oceans of what I owe to each) to the three pillars of kindness and generosity upon which this book rests: to Richard Howard, for prompting, enabling and improving so of what is here, for believing so forcefully in the work and me, and for urging the book into the world; Thomas Healy for irreplaceable friendship, support of all kinds, and being the constant and exemplary reader-over-my-shoulder; and Joanne Park, for collaboration on the Korean translation, and without whom nothing.

"Of Mere Virtuosity" and "Biblios" are for Richard.

"On the Reason of Forms and Qualities" and "Were Less" are for Lucie.

"Circe's Wand" and "Belshazzar's Feast" are for Tom.

"Cloister," "Souvenir of Sunchon," and "Adultery" are for Joanne.

"Tenebrae" is in memory of my mother.

I

Die Mühle Brennt—Richard
(*After a painting by Georg Bazelitz*)

When the red chair suspended in air
grazes the top of your head
and the white pitcher that rests on the chair

neither falls nor spills, you will move
to the window, or the empty space
in the wall left by the guns on the hill

just outside the city, and be amazed
at the mill ablaze in the distance,
the loud report of dry beams knuckled

under heat, the carousel of shadows spun
around the orange center of the flames,
because you know this cannot happen here

or because you know the mill's been on fire
for so long that the city's been consumed
entirely, and the heat from the mill

has blistered the red paint on the chair
and dried the water from the pitcher,
and, if you wait one more instant,

afraid that it is too late, it will be too late,
and the chair and pitcher will drift
through your hair as ash.

II

Aria: *Lascia ch'io pianga*

Light from the courtyard at 3 A.M.
and Raphael's flying on his bed again.

September of seraphs and black holes,
cabals urging their blue volts, lithium

itineraries for the heights of Mount Sinai,
and apotropaic stacks of books bedside—

carts with weasel voices wheel down the
hall. We have a plan. . . .
                              And this but one

I listen to tonight, and not the worst—
oracles and auricular proofs from the lost

Pleiad, the unsolved absence left
in the ward. I want to hear Handel.

April's sweet liquid is snow; the bathed veins
nictitate with ice. I want a dissolve: to

go mapless to the mountain's top
and step past salt and cloud into pure voice.

Cavafy Suite

1. These Walls

With no consideration, pity, or shame,
they built their walls around me, thick and high.
The city lay eclipsed, the sky hemmed tight
into a small, dim vowel. What stood outside
would always stand outside, and stone
was home. I had had so much to do. Now
I think of nothing else: words unmoored, ghost
caravels in arctic mists with phantom crews.
How could I not have noticed anything?
I never heard the builders, not a sound,
as imperceptibly they closed me in,
never saw the trail of footprints leading
from the quarry where the last block was cut
to here, the center where the shadows thin.

2. These Windows

In the still center where the shadows thin,
then fatten on the empty days and rooms,
I wander round and round and try to find
the windows rumored in these walls. I've heard
the moonlight compass arc the stones, seen wind
pool beside the bed; I know they're there, know
all will change when the clipped footfalls
lead to the sill littered with heron's wings.
Still day eats day like kine in pharaohs' dreams,
and I can't find that whole note in the wall
where the awful inside is no longer all.
Perhaps it's better if I don't. Who knows
the tyranny of gravity and sun—
who knows what the daylight will expose?

3. Shoulder

What did I reach for on the middle shelf—
an album I'd wanted to look at wedged
between the two I thought I'd thrown away—
when the bandage came undone? What did I say
I'd done? Banged up against the wall,
fallen, measuring jalousies, from the sill?
You saw the blood melt down and the cut
open a corridor that led to promised
false-absolving wards, saw a longitude
of darknesses. You cleaned and patched it up
again. Old gauze, that clotted scroll you'd meant
to throw in the garbage but happily forgot
on the chair you haven't sat in since, I've kept
shelved behind those red morocco bindings.

4. In Camera

Call it an imperfection in the lens.
An iris stem bends in the half-filled glass
and bends again: the solving dissolution.
From what my hands have done, from what I've been,
you will learn everything of what I'm not.
Memory dipped in red and the cooling tub;
then summer of footprints on the moon
when the sky fell in—penultimate disaster—
and I saw not myself, nor rose from here.
And still the heart is hard; no leave is granted.
My eyes in the mask behind the veil are film
where negative figures coil, their lightness swapped
for dark. These chimeras, this silent cinema,
this thing of darkness I acknowledge mine.

5. Days of 1996

Thirsting for dryness, I went to Marrakech
that spring I was engaged, then quit my job,
then, disengaged, climbed down into Sinai.
Proscription in prescription: the law on tablets
of salt seeding the dark, like sodium lamps
spent on the uptown puddles—
offer of a covenant in lightning bolts.
There were debts and things that couldn't be undone.
What serves now is what I have preserved,
and not the preservation but the breaking:
tablets piecemeal at the mountain's base,
dark eyes, dark bodies in the dark medina,
gold medallion of a Barbary macaque,
this wandering tongue, a desert miracle.

6. The God Abandons

The final pleasure: listen to the voices,
in Spanish, Creole, and the salsa muted
from the station down the hall, the music
of some strange procession. At midnight
invisible taxis rush down Fifth Avenue,
No lies, no lies. I will not mourn; I was
prepared too long. He abandons; I let go,
his capsule angels tongued, spat out, and flushed.
The city he'd forgiven me—its palm-vaulted
boulevards, its level walks—is now foreclosed.
I must listen louder, above all taxis, must ask
from him behind the curtain and tender him
nothing. Only take the narrow fall
to the farther city—shrill and obsidian.

7. Outskirts

Are you astonished at what I'm doing now?
or even that I am? So long your look and touch
were Schliemann rummaging Ionian dust
for ruins, charred Apollos, bronze lamenting
a scurry of gods and godlikes on the plain.
Your oracles are stillborns brined in jars
I keep on the sill. No Troy: Columbia Heights,
Pelham. I sift for ghosts again—the claimed,
the ones by right. From the elevated No. 6
ratcheting across the Bronx, I see two piers,
black and spiny as urchins, collapsing down
a bank, and a pair of swans improbably chalked
on the slate of river, large with disaster
or a longer music, necks in question marks.

8. More Windows

The lions rest and watch Fifth Avenue and
let me pass. A block up, waiting for the light,
I watch the windows of Nat Sherman's store—
"tobacconist to the world"—below the wooden
headdressed Indians and the broken clock,
where a phantom city plashes and rolls by
like a sea god's phalanxes of dolphins
escorting to his bed a Nereid.
And there you are—astonished to a stop,
and I'm stone still in the surge, let slip
by the changing signal. So long away,
and yet what can we do but flag a cab,
too busy with uncertain hands and lips
to tell the driver where we want to go.

Lot's Wife

Just the susurrus of bare citrus trees crossed
by winds unscrolling down ravined hillsides,
but I thought, in that infinite moment
when I turned, that I heard them call.
Then nothing, no sound, but the sight
of those branches—or were they penitent arms—
like veins of ice within a gelling sea,
gone pale in the fierce white sky, and then
there was nothing at all. All that was our city
and our friends, the brine and stench of the fishmongers'
stalls, and the complaint of wagons' tongues
in the thick-trafficked streets, was the empty
space that bloomed upon the plain;
and the detritus of their tears—this lump
of salt on the outbound path—I am.

And it is the terrible thing that's happened
before: my hand as heavy as marble and chalky
against the glass, the white capsules—those pills
of mitigating salt—scattered on the bed;
the dark street below is salted with headlights,
and in the park sodium lamps hum in cocoons
of light, disclosing updrafts of moths.
Failure of which, of faith, of hope,
of love, the whole triumvirate? I turn and freeze,
and turn and burn again, in a shell game of self,
turn away from or toward I cannot tell,
to take just one or just to take them all.

Were Less

Were weary
of werewolf moons,

of weather, its chalcedony hands,
heavy and cold, its wet

changes, and winter seepage
through the welded roof

of a willed if not wished
wellness, and its whispering

witnesses in the wainscoting,
of whether to

or not: were wary
of water, the deep pools by the weir,

where body's weight
was wirgeld to be paid for waste:

were wept
by west winds, ears and eyes

wincing like icicles on the eaves
of use: were weary

of wander, of wake
to wonder where I was

or who:
were waiting:

were washed
from the hands of words,

wanton-voweled,
wending their way Styx-ward,

waving *adieu, adieu,* and the world
whirled down in their wake: were

warned: were
whelmed by ward, by watch

of the whiteness of the wall:
were wrapped

in wicker, in wax,
and whisked away

by women with wolfsbane
eyes, in whaleboned gowns,

and waned:
were less

or more or less
less and less,

the leased self,
subtraction by addition,

the double and double-tongued
I: were wanting,

will be wanting,
winter into winter,

warrant, a waiver of tense,
of saw-toothed consonant

auxiliaries, always
wanting *am*,

wanting always
more.

The Rothko Digression

You hand me the book, an old gray grammar
from the mildewed box, and say, *Now say
what shouldn't be said.* The binding splits
open to a middle chapter with an exercise
that drills "I did" and eliminates "I done."
It's called "the game of policeman" and goes
like this: *In room X, a disorderly character
has made a mess; you call a policeman
to come and arrest him at once.
The policeman enters the room and says,
"James, did you do that?" "Not I," says James,
"I did not do it. Perhaps Lawrence did it."
"Lawrence did you do that?" "No, I did not . . ."
and so on, until at last the last one asked
confesses, "I did it." "You did (not done)
a disorderly act; now go and sit
in the corner of the room."* So then, what
is it I shouldn't say? The nameless purple
flower that unpetals on James, the father,
the policeman's chest? (*James, did you
do that? I did not do it. Who is to blame?*)

I will say only what can be said, give you
the game in measured lines, and leave it
at that, take my medicine, and find a tale,
say one from Genesis, of the mistook
backward glance, to wash it down;

I will transcribe, translate, matter closer
to farther bones. So, at the running
of the day-in, day-out montage of service
revolvers, plump as crows, and when
the bright-edged remnants of wineglasses
rehearse arcs just below my hands,
I will tell you something more like this:
This way I walk through the large white gallery,
around the axis of a spiraled stair,
where Rothko's final paintings line the walls,
so elegant and sad and beautiful,
that say, "The dark is always at the top,"
and "Mine is a bitter old age"–say "Incised
and self-inflicted wounds," say "Exsanguination."
Which is not bad but is quite beside the point.

Normandy
(*Virginia Woolf, 1939*)

Carnac

"Pavilioned in the fields of France": at last
it rains; the little Brides—communiquées—troop by,
white under their black umbrellas. The past
is tastable. (I won't say L is satisfied
with Breton food; we've hit some wretched inns.)
We sat among the druid tombs all day:
stones like giant hives or washerwomen
balancing white sheets upon their heads.
A siege of herons blanketed the quays;
by the river, old men in black velvet
marched with bagpipes, and cuckoos snapped.
What I write today I will not write again.
Do we even exist save on the lips of friends,
white boats lost against the white-capped sea?

Concarneau

Like white boats lost on the white-capped sea,
we meandered town to town, Vannes, then Les Rochers;
now here at Concarneau, since yesterday.
The drive was low sand hills, troops of pines, gray leas,
old gray farms, and against the charcoal bay
the green translucent stands of corn. Bees droned
like aeroplanes around the hives. Auray
was beautiful: old walls, blue fishing boats.
No news worth much but talk of war; they say
that it must come next month. There is a general
madness in the air. Much tired, Dearest,
and now no word from you? The sea is feral,

white-capped like Gauguin's Breton girls. We cross
on Tuesday next. I, and the world, feel old.
It's rapturous here, and civilized, but cold.

Bayeux
Cold, but rapturous and civilized:
mornings bees drone like sinful thoughts
about the bishop's mitre of a beehive
past the courtyard wall. We saw a fishing boat
blessed today, a man in white in a palanquin
of gold and stars. The tobacconist says
he's descended from the Bishop of Dublin.
Midsummer's night, I'm half tipsy. Girls with lace
caps like Eiffel Towers under a great triangle
of Japanese lanterns: I need to write these,
not the words that must be said. No news, a little
talk of Gertler's suicide. Each day, the whipped sea
makes pentimenti of Dover, and I forget to rest.
One can scarcely bear it. Only we must.

Envoi
Even we must, if one can scarcely bare it:
the river again, old men in black velvet,
the tired air, the madness of Japanese
lanterns. Dearest, do I need to write this?

Well-ness

Foot-deep gray sediment,
blue bottlenecks, pipe stems,
and bones, a pediment
of oyster shells in the hoop

of stone, long lost (the house
mortgaged to flame) beneath
Victorian paving blocks:
now under glass, a lapse

in the sidewalk on Pearl,
the round, dry walls bask
in the astonishment of day.
I've known that infiltration,

that roof of ground, and wakened
to an archaeology's
alarm, the several suns
of white robes in corridors.

Does the well hold, too,
in its nautilus hollow,
antique percussion
of the pushed-back shore,

that prophesy estuarial
sibilants and a thirst
for a cold dark water
where the eyeless feed?

Split Decision

Half-
hearted night thunder
over the too-familiar
Albinoni adagio—
rain pills on the wrought-
iron fire
escape—

Whole
again, says the amber
vial of salts—*Home again,*
says the capsule of morning,
the prescribed and proscribed
both so relentlessly
light—

A Discoverie of the Bermoodas

Look there, at the edge where the world drops off:

You can see them kirtled
in white crepe, the sand
and palm-draped backs of slumbering
leviathans, gorged on cashiered prophets
and the endless deep—

the Isles of Shipwrecks, the Isles of Devils,
their bays abristle with half-sunk masts
and the air with gutturals and gongs.
Always the wanting waves come in and in
and find them empty.

Going there I think of almost never.

Out of Egypt

Shall it be said the gain is small
for him who entrusts himself
to your will, Beloved, Son of Re?

So long. And now sun's slag,
thick fingers, unheld breaths,
camel stench, and so many words.

I am not here.
Take this leathery husk,
the friable guts, and the panel

set against my feet, painted
with a view into the temple—
banded columns, pediments

with spread falcon's wings
—take me. These will avail you
nothing who cannot see

yourselves to me at the portal
within portals, deep in the picture
worth a thousand worlds.

Make of them what you will—
even another, past words, embalmed
in salts, with the tell-all chart

at the foot of his bed,
and ward receding into ward.
I will be there neither.

III

Of Mere Virtuosity

How long the scrims of his mother's eyes
were fulgent with the old city
up in flames, for which her kind

would suffer blame (and would
for every corpse disposed
obscurely in divers fragments

by the wharves), and flickered
with recall of Guy Fawkes days,
pope and devil effigies alight

and live cats sewn in their bellies
yowling the lexicons of hell.
Language was his phoenix rising

from such ashes. But she's been dead
ten years. He had expected
little in that winter, no music.

Handel, wracked with paralytic
fits, threatened in Hanoverian
accents of spending a year abroad,

and yet as February rattles
the trivia stalls, the voices come,
an undisguised lightning, among

the fine ladies and *petits maîtres,*
full of terror and astonishment.
Trussed in his stiff canvas bodice,

late swaddled or too soon mummified,
the migraine detonating
behind his eyes, he watches

Semele in a gold headdress,
set with lapis birds-of-paradise,
gold robe trailing like a comet's tail,

totter from her bed to the footlights,
still mortal and insensible
of any change. Will-o'-the wisps

fly off the candent mirror
in her hand. As she stands at the brink
of the stage, her air rises slowly

through the house, wrapping itself
in the gilt décor, a new perfection,
life consuming, burning his eaten bones

to the cinders of redress, from which
we can never take any less than
the fired plumage of full excess.

Weldon Kees

The parking lot was empty: I could sit
As I'd practiced a dozen days and watch
The bay go blue and tangerine and botched
Night give the upper hand to day, outwit
The urgent voices, drive away, and quit
All expectation; I could see a thatched
Beach hut, Baja, a life semidetached
From bridges, love, from all my preterite
And mortgaged words. I knew it could be done.
And yet the old man waving from his cell
As we pulled out of St. Elizabeth's
Would not let go of me. That was a hell
That made anodyne any death.
I had no other life. I wanted none.

Tenebrae

1. Leaving England

When asked, she would prefer to tell
About her sister's rescue from Norway,
The night after the Germans seized Oslo:
The truck ride into Sweden, the long way
Home across Siberia, the Pacific,
The States, with their father who would write
About it all. But pressed she'd recollect
The pitch-dark pitching steamer lighting
Out of the harbor, blacked-out Liverpool
A hulked-up null behind, and her mother squeezed
Into her bunk, reciting Noyes and de la Mare.
Gone now, but ask her anyway: Is there ease
On your new voyage or anyone to tell?
I'll listen and say to the dark "The Listeners."

2. Long Island

"The house of unripe figs," Bethpage, named for
The town where Christ procured the ass he rode
Into Jerusalem, and once itself known
As Jerusalem, once home to pickle farms
And factories on Whitman's fish-shaped island—
A place to leave the city for. She spent the first
Week hacking down the firs and hedge out front,
Clearing out what would become her garden:
Bulbs of narcissi, irises, Stars-of-Holland,
Daylilies, glads; each year a nursery tub
Of annuals, sweet Williams, pinks, primroses;
White peonies against the gray wood siding.
Last year I rode the train out there—the house,
Now yellow, hooped in a ruin of shrubs.

3. 1969

Summer of miracles, the pennant stretch,
Seaver and Koosman all but unhittable,
We watched the moon dust breached
(Our town where they'd built the lunar module).
What was the opposite of miracle?
More and more frequent stays in the city,
Medics puzzling the muscles' loss of will;
They thought she was dying, and I was sitting
In the dark in sunlit rooms; neither
Given a name for what went wrong, betrayed
By something of ourselves, no cures
In the offing. We were knit together
By unraveling. Dying once, she weighed
Her body's loss; the loss this time I learn.

4. Legerdemain

I asked her if it was a sin to abet
(Vide *Dragnet*) a runaway, and she knew
There was a runaway (in prep school blues;
As far from Manhattan as he could get
With lunch funds on the L.I.R.R.), in that
Omniscient-mother way. In flight herself,
She'd sought a quiet life, a faith, apart
From the hothouse of intellect, bookshelved
Emotions, where she grew but didn't thrive.
Then I in an arc reversing hers. Pushing
The envelope of what bound us till it stretched
To the world's other side. Still she contrived,
In her magician's repertoire, to ring
The globe, her heart in its seven-league boots.

5. A Widow's Dream

Telling him through the half-year courtship
Everything she wanted and believed,
His quiet taken for assent; she let slip
Once she felt she'd been deceived.
But long companioned to that vacancy
She can not feel slighted or perturbed
When, six months dead, he climbs
The cellar stairs and comes without a word
Into her room. Newspaper bleeds
From the bullet hole in his chest.
He rifles through the closet like a thief
And hangs an iron chain around her neck,
Then leaves. She reaches to him, but her hands
Are locked in the middle drawer of the bedstand.

6. St. Clare

Bedridden, in her final illness, Clare
Watched as Christmas midnight mass was said
In Francis's basilica on the far
Side of Assisi; named then the patron saint
Of television. In the end the TV's
All that she can manage; even the longed-for
Visits are too much. I tried to read her
The Coleridge she'd read to me at three
(I in the tub for days to cool the fever
Penicillin flared), but she could only sleep.
Convert out of her father's house, decades
Of obscure sickness, the cloister of the home:
Two Clares so wed. In her absence I come
Into a vow: this the privilege of perfect poverty.

7. Albany

I had been away a year and would be gone
Again until the fall. The likelihood
That she'd not last that long we left unsaid.
"Don't send books. I can't read any longer.
The tapes are nice, though." That afternoon we wrote
Her letters. "No one's washed my hair all week.
There's a can of dry shampoo your sister brought
Here somewhere. Could you?" A dinner cart squeaked
Down the corridor. Her frail head almost bare,
I held it like an infant's, breakable, and combed.
"Remember how you used to brush my hair
When you were little?" "Yes. Do you know
Elizabeth Bishop's poem 'Shampoo'?"
"No." "It's a love poem. I'll send it to you."

8. The Woman Who Loved Robert Donat

We watched *Spellbound* and tried hard not to laugh
At the Dalí dreams and cure in the bat
Of an eyelash (even if it were *her* lash);
Peck and Bergman rushing for their train. . . .
This spring they mounted a relic of old Penn
Station outside our school: a faceless "Day,"
Green-graffitied, salvaged from Jersey fens.
We would have passed it often on our way
In from the Island, for the gentle dentist
She would not give up and appeasements,
The hall of dinosaurs, the Met's steeled knights.
Two fugitives, two reluctant spies. . . . Then
On our next-to-last night, *The 39 Steps*
(Tell me, Mr. Memory). More trains. More flight.

9. Leaving

The obscenity of funeral eloquence
And open casket, the impossible
Task of packing her few things in two small
Boxes to take home from the home, now distanced
By thirty thousand feet and the elsewhere
Thrum of jet engines. On pale blue airmail
Paper, her last letter, never mailed:
"Kelly made the honor roll. I hear
Paul and Marge are off to Colorado.
A friend of mine has brought me yellow tulips.
Your brother wrote this for me, Mom." Nothing
To say *My lungs won't last the week.* Below
In the sun, the tapered Finger Lakes flare up,
Then are extinguished by the airplane's wing.

"Somewhere Off the Coast of Brazil"
(*Elizabeth Bishop, 1951*)

"I see you in this dining room–saloon,
a scotch and soda tilting in your fist;
you stand one-legged, heron-wise, then list
against the bar. The freighter's small. At noon
our sad young missionary will appear
with wife and sons. . . . Far south, beyond Brazil,
below the cold convergence, where frazil,
floebergs, and breccia—sea ice—and sheer
white mists well up like Antarctic tears,
I sometimes think would be the place to go. . . .
But your thin face particulates to snow;
you're still in Europe, will be all next year.
I worry how too well we play at ghosts.
We disembark tomorrow at Santos."

The Inn on the Road to Bemerton

A single candle flame, the yellow twin
of the cathedral's spire visible
today across the plain, dark dolphin's fin
on Salisbury's green sea, and compline bells—

and all that's lit is Jane's face and the girl's,
both bent in prayer, a pigeons' burble, then
a darkness absolute. The pamphlet furled
in my cold hand—the woodcuts of three men

at Colchester chained amid redressing flames—
that the carter thrust on me this afternoon
burns darker still: the ink and ash of names,
ours to forget or not forget, not soon.

The rafters swallow shadow into shade,
and make the babel rising from downstairs
spend questions that can never be repaid.
The lingering book I study is of air.

I have acquired painfully my doubts.
Tomorrow we'll be in Bemerton by nones,
but early, with the drovers we'll go out
to watch the sun come up on the great stones.

Regeneration

The shroud he kept in the middle drawer,
Unwashed, perfumed with the damp
Of the church vault where he lay the week
Before his soul returned. He never
Spoke of what had happened then,
But muttered, *The light, the light,*
When the bells were rung for matins, nones,
And vespers. He never blinked; somehow
We knew it was heaven, not hell,
Who had sent him back to us. He never
Touched his tools again, or wife. He spent
The days immersing himself in freezing water
And letting his garments dry on him all night.
When asked how he bore it, he replied,
I have seen a greater cold.

The Death Hunters

The smell of it had crept into morning—
not that you would notice, but we did,
woke, and made our way out of the wood.
Under the first gray languets of day
we could make out a spire on the hill—
then the bells, then a low keening
that wooled the fields as thickly as spring fog
(it was late March, St. Dismas' Eve and cold)
and might have been the women or the wind,
or the one who'd gone and could not yet let go.

We didn't need to ask which house it was;
as always, once we'd made the road,
a kind of gravity drew us in,
as dumb as salmon up white-shouldered falls.
In the borrowed dark of the shuttered room
he had been washed already and laid out.
Some crumbs and wax drops wept across his chest:
the sin-eater had passed through in the night.
We set our buffets—the small black stools—
beside the door, balanced his box on them,

and brought the crown outside for hymns,
then led them with the corse to the churchyard.
The keening started up again. I could not turn,

and still it seemed to me it came not from
the stunned ones in our wake but from the clefts
of the yew trees, and was not so much lament
as an oracle. We crossed the bridge where half
a dozen crones stood on the banks to harvest
the water over which we passed—a balm
bottled for the stricken and the dying.

Myself, I'll not of it when the time comes.

On the Reason of Forms and Qualities
Transported from the Antique French,
Being an Apologie as Lately Meditated
in Riverside Park upon the Occasion
of Inquiry from a Dissenter

For it has grown cold, and
therefore we must convene in
two times threes. For ice from
the north sheathes the river,
indistinguishable
from the flour mixed with

water, the death's heads, moths
devouring bridal
veils, the bridal veils,
the unveiled brides,
the shroud devouring
moths and brides, and the ash-

full smoke. (You're there with your
cigarette—remade in
the river, the puddle,
the brass railing, these two
eyes, and the mirror you
pull from your purse with a

roll of fifties—await
the hyperdactylic
vender of opiates
loping through the park.) For
it is growing colder,
and we must have light, must

distinguish which water
is which, have something dry,
hammer out a moon and
sun, have fish on Friday,
must play with mud. For it
shall be coldest, dearest,

and we must rest, but if
we mouth it right again
and again, and this once
more than we count on
one hand, the extinguished
river will crack the ice,

and trees in the park will
unveil as brides, breathing
moths in each vulgate gasp.

Sijo
(After Franz Wright)

Well, I've visited,   too, stars on foot,
               barefoot, that is   alone and not,
The path there,   its bruited milky way,
               is brittle glass   admixed with salt.
What remains,   the night's work down here,
               is all tweezers   and iodine.

Nonesuch

Weight of ivory under my fingers—
        themselves past ivory, past pearl,
             almost transparent, five

distant icicles that sometimes puddle
        almost to a fist, sometimes seem
             to remember to be mine—I feel,

but know the piano's touch
        is dust-bound down the hall. The fly
             at the window is Father's violin,

or sometimes Gould at Carnegie abuzz
        above the aria da capo; sometimes
             a fly; sometimes the phone—all music now.

It could be elsewhere or elsewhen—
        or what they tell me is here, is now,
             a place whose borderlines are drawn

in snow—I see a map of the world
        pinned to the wall, whose longitudes
             refuse to bend and meld, whose

southern continent seems without end.
        The meridians and parallels
             that chart the terra cognita of my limbs

are lost, and the stars are helmeted
        in fog. I'm past the convergence, and more
                and more become my own Antarctica:

I follow a trail across the ice, toward a pole
        reported but unmarked where white
                extinguishes in white, and what

the ice retains it will not yield,
        not even to Bach. For west is forever
                here and there is no east.

IV

Straight, No Chaser

Outside Los Dos Amigos barbershop
the dealers' favorite phone hangs off the hook
and sways, as if at the other end of the line
someone's playing remastered Ellington
or Monk, nocturnes for the break of day.
A warm breeze cruises the Heights, down

to the underpass and toward the river.
Last night's snow is disappearing fast,
the sidewalk brilliantined with melt in lieu
of the usual piss or spit or spunk;
rock salt crunches underfoot like empty
vials on the stoop behind the high wrought-

iron gate. Where you head toward Broadway,
in the diminished curbside snowbank,
one very large blue woman's shoe aims
its heel at the sun, its toe still buried.
A flying plastic grocery bag festoons,
for a moment, the bare gingko—then lets go.

At Hart Crane's Grave

If I touch your hand do I touch your lips,
inside of the knee, is all skin one, cells talking
to each other? If, then this river (not a river)
here, steel dark, corrugated, coruscant

with the lights of downtown and cruise boats,
below the bridge, his bridge, a gray
concretion of waves, is yet his grave,
one with the green and turquoise stream

that laved and shrouded him north of Havana.
The swirl of phosphorescent water once
and again there, a spiral galaxy, might still contain
a molecule of his dissolute remains

as once his resolute brain could have lodged
in gray the original atom of the world.
Long shots, yes, but so is what we do with words:
his, these, yours (*I'm cold, come home with me*),

demanded on this Brooklyn promenade.
What can outstay the bridge, outrun the water?

In the Labyrinth

Across the bridge, and even at this hour,
headlit white threads of traffic ravel down

into Manhattan. Your kiss harbors
a Chlorox smell; we both could use a shower

and some sleep, but head for Battery Park
to watch the day arrive. Past Exchange,

we come up face to muzzle with the great
black bull, and leaning on its flank

you double-dare me to go down on you
again right then, right there. The lighting sky

tips the horns in red. This color, the wet
on my fingertips, the redolence of immanent rain:

how these outpromise you, your black-
sailed words, your rigged ship riding at anchor.

Cloister

Still winter translates phantoms from my breath,
And spring with its glib greens, its shibboleth
Of birth, renewal, all that shit, evades
These gardens and transplanted colonnades;
A red sky tightropes on the Palisades.
Two blank postcards: one a Merovingian
Gold cup, the other Carolingian,
A reliquary of St. Porphyry.
What can I write you, love? Mere *agape*,
And "How is school, your husband, and your son?"
When even in this monkish walk, all done
And said, to all ears what I would confess,
Is how, like Occam's razor through the mess
Of language, marriage, and geographies
That yet consign us to antipodes,
Your taste, the myrrh and chrism of you wet
Anoints my lips, your missive, my gazette?

Souvenir of Sunchon

Sheaves of drying sesame and an ancient
Schwinn, a dead russet hen strapped to its rack,
leaned against the red clay walls, and every
horizontal surface blazed in the sun

With drying peppers; the narrow plain
tessellated by the balks of flush rice fields,
white egrets stood like chessmen in the flood,
and ginseng cloistered in black-tented rows.

There where the river skirted the Kaya Mountains,
we found the Silla Buddha we'd hunted for,
its lotus pedestal and the worn folds of its robe
barely discernable, slender torso and plump

cupped hands, the limestone face half gone.
During the Koryo dynasty, farmers
would bring their children here—the ones
feared mute who had not learned to speak.

Touch the statue, and before the moon
is out, your tongue will be released.
Rilke says that when a traveler returns,
what he carries is some word he's gained,

and all that we may be intended for
is to say words, say *river, mountain, stone.*
Gang. San. Dohl. Here by the sullen Hudson,
the Riverside sycamores bicker in night winds,

and I am trying to recall two other words—
one for the smell of your hair, one for the small
of your back touched as you climbed a stair—
a stone kept from your river in my hand.

Eros

Near, nearing, not alighting, circling
at a distance that means nothing,
lost in gelid distances from here.
But it is enough for safety, to orbit
in unbetrayed silence, in the dark,
and send back photographs of what
could readily be mistaken for
a Cycladic figurine or a saurian
bone, a moon face airless, pocked
by collisions with lesser asteroids.
In close-ups, note the many grooves,
scars that run for miles, may be related
to fractures below the surface. They're in
the *Times;* I'll leave it out for you tonight.

Light Red over Black
(*A painting by Mark Rothko*)

Another woman, now in your room,
with movie star's breasts, laughs in a photograph.

Some other girl, now in your dream,
curls up asleep on the pillow of your arm.

Someday, in the fields where we used to play,
wild azaleas will bloom:

when pages, thumbed illegible
in my memory, open at random,
a red-eyed sun will plunge to scumbled hills.

Take from this picture the frame ablaze,
what is dyed black in exsanguination:

I would go to you
Shedding my few fierce drops.

                              −Choi Young-Mi
                    (translated from the Korean)

Mausoleum

Black lozenges, the unburdened
yet heavier hearse and limousines,
roll back down the tongue of hill

in a hide-and-seek among the yews
and bleached geometries
of tombs and headstones.

The bronze doors grate;
a slap of absolute darkness,
then resolution to olive gray

sufficient to make clear
the corridor. Here narrow
drawers with the black bones

of those that went in manuscript
up in flames, unvoiceable.
Here plain wooden casks

for the natural deaths:
forscrifen, farsed, cony-catch'd.
And, farther on, monuments

for the worn to death,
an angel for *angel;*
iron boxes for aged argots;

alabaster urns for the ones
that simply shriveled up:
dainty, chrysoprase,

forlorn, and *alabaster.*
A niche in perpetual
slippage into shadow where

gloaming and *darkling* ghost
away. Then here, near the end,
a small and private vault,

where I've laid those words
I had for second-person singular,
first-person plural, a name,

a word that was lied
too well, and two tongues
of indistinguishable dust.

Belshazzar's Feast

"I just don't buy it when Richard
says that he never did it, that bit
about the sea his sole embrace. . . ."

"What's unrisked is perfect, if unproved,
and, knowing he would fail, too much
to lose. . . ." "But all that touching,

kissed soldiers in his arms. . . ."
"The dead are easy, love without
consequences, and the dying don't say no."

So on we'd go all night: of Whitman
and our work, over the bad French covers
of soft rock and the better steak *au poivre*

at Métisse, you wondering where I
and the living were in my lines, and all
of us half in love with the you in yours.

Then underground, at West 110th,
the uptown local missed by seconds:
the wrack in the thick wet between the ties

quavers in the back draft. Orange-vested
linemen emerge from between the beams,
resume their tapping way along the rails,

half a dozen good graybeards, tracing
the windrow on Long Island's shore
amid the sea's refusals. What do you want

from me then, that I grew up there,
in the gut of his piscine island,
of the covenants unmade there

and the long commitment since to lying
low. Twin yellow lines stretch out
along the tracks from the tunnel's mouth,

and two questions converge
like those trails of light. I would tell you
this orange strip at the platform's edge

is what shore I know, and is all
you need to know. I would insist, Let
me have what's here, these things alone,

and let that be enough. Let me not
have done what I should, and that
be enough. These things and me,

their inviolate confusion: the strew
of urban artifacts and the man asleep there
on the bench, his head wrapped

in a subway guide, mapped
like a phrenologist's specimen.
But the harsh headlights of a 9

bend into view. Not in service,
it waddles past with a clatter
that says *numbered, weighed,*

and *wanting.* And I'm left facing
the tiled wall, the sign that reads
NO CLEARING IN THE NICHE.

Batfowling
(*Central Park*)

It was our time; we heard the owl
leave its Norway spruce and circle
twice above Dendur, then plummet mouse-

ward through the shadow-purled
pinetum. A last red hiccup
of twilight. The great maps unfurled

across the lawn, and we came up
from our cave. Unspoken
water was set out in white cups

on an overgrown stone bench;
we drank and set to work,
untying the long nets, woven

from strings of widows' clavichords,
a widow's cruse of widows' weeds,
and weeds and great willow herb.

We loved the dark, the trees;
we shunned the drives, the lamps
in their light farthingales, and steered

our velocipedes across the grass
to the appointed gates. We made
good time, and soon the nets were cast

in catenary swoops from maple
to hemlock, pin oak to elm,
Cleopatra's needle to fake

castle, falconer to angel
troubling the waters. The sky, freighted
with counterglow, zodiacal

and city light, as if surrendered
to Olbers' paradox, was sinking
into day. The nets were playing

remembered madrigals, and we knew
that, in a moment, as they rose—
the skeins of geese, the great blue

herons, mottled pigeons, sparrows,
blackbirds, runaway macaws, jays,
a wedge of swans, and ghosts

from scores of plowed-under graves—
they would be ours. Their voices we'd rebraid
into our voice, and an hour later

the nets would serve as well to take
the unglued stars (they'd be our eyes) as they
dove terribly toward the lake.

V

To the Honorable Members of the Taliban Council

Astonished with body hewn
from the living rock, flesh and robes
finished in mud and straw, I stood

where the long silk bolts of sky
unrolled above the valley,
where my gilded face would summon

pilgrims from the spice-trade roads
scrolling out to Cathay and the west,
to climb the sandstone cliff, honeycombed

with sanctuaries, to the burning
sandalwood, the walls aflame
with the painted thingness of things.

He who sees the law sees me;
He who sees me sees the law.
And now, my Councilors, you men

of law, you disembody me, refine
me by mortar fire down to dust,
to a constellation of shell holes in the stone.

Later, when men's lives extend
for eighty thousand years and their height
reaches more than eighty feet,

I will reappear, towering
over them, and with my toe
shatter the mountain's rock.

An old disciple will emerge,
his small bones wrapped in cascading
saffron robes, and mount the air

like the yellow-winged garuda bird
—as his one body manifests
a thousand bodies, fountains

of fire tumbling from his feet,
water flaming from his head—
to slip into the cleft sky

and be gone. Then for their sakes
I will speak. What was hidden
in dross will shine in purity,

the veil of ignorance removed,
and this riven cliff,
its rubble and enshrined pockmarks,

your ship of state's engraved
manifest of ruin, will become again
the fixed point, the auspicious place.

The Other Hand

One year in Lent as he was praying, his arms outstretched, a blackbird settled in his palm, built a nest, and laid an egg in it. Kevin waited until the tiny bird had hatched and fledged before he moved.

—Courtney Davis, *The Celtic Saints*

And on the other hand—the balance
of Kevin that stays inside, attends
to the business that was at hand

when the unlooked-for blackbird,
a negative votive flame,
lit on the upturned palm

outside—nests fixed shades
of the far side of the cell,
damp, and the heavy cold

that bends the hand to the slate.
Cramp curls his fingers;
phosphorescent mold

grows apace with the hatchlings.
A tail's eelish pass, exploratory
nips. In time, Kevin resumes

left-off devotions, reclaims
the weathered hand, unburdened,
light. But the other hand still

weighs the empty space,
basalt, ovate and absolute,
which will, he knows, begin

to multiply like the miracle
salmon once fetched to him
by an otter for his hungry

acolytes and seemed
at the time more than enough
to satisfy a world.

Ad Astra
(1929–30)

There a friend of Barby's, Blair Hughes-Stanton, a book illustrator, met them and drove Lawrence up to the sanatorium, a large multistory chalet with the unfortunate name of Ad Astra, perched on a hilltop a thousand feet above the Mediterranean.
—Brenda Maddox, *D. H. Lawrence: The Story of a Marriage*

1. September
Here we are again, and it's marvelous,
So glad we're back, so glad to see the sea.
So lovely here. The house is wonderfully
In air, bang in the sun. The eucalyptus
Trees, so tressy once, are sawn to stumps,
And the garden is parsed in stones—a grizzling
Of the north, its disenchantments, the puzzling
Medics seeding me with arsenic. But the unkempt
Palms blister with fresh green. And it's so still—
The sea so still and autumn slate blue.
Men sit motionless by their dark nets. From here
One can feel Africa. (Coming up the hill,
Embroidered in pipe smoke, is the Greek, our new
Gardener.) I'm better. We'll go there next year.

71

2. October

We're up along the cliffs toward the pines
Where bulbs were thrown away and late narcissi
Ember now. Send my red dictionary
With the typewriter and the gramophone;
There's a room for you this winter if you come.
When will I be there again? God knows. *There* seems
As far away as Nineveh, and that a dream
In sand, and the running sand a dream of home.
The cycle of the greater year goes round
And as it turns will probably bring me back.
One has to wait for the auspicious day.
I find I lean on destiny now that I've found
My will so curbed by illness, its attack
That runs upon me in red-winged waves.

3. November

Was I gone again? I must have been. Shadows flare
From the mantel as enormous blue gentians,
The cold hands of dead Illyrian kings
Slip under my vest, and twilight stares
From a face—a desiccated hornet's nest
Hung in the mirror—that I hesitate over,
Then reclaim. Outside the mistral clamors
In the pines. When will this resting turn to rest
At last? Down by the sardine boats a single gull
Dives again and again against the sea
As if Icarus in a Keystone comedy.
The cook left pomegranates in the hall.
If I ate them all, that eternity of seeds,
Would the dark ground open then and marry me?

4. December

In bed again. I do not work unless
You call poems work. But no use dying yet.
The sea bursts on the island opposite
In chrysanthemums and lions' manes. Caresse
Is back in Paris with a silver jar
Of ashes. The moon, her poisoned arrows
Are against us. What strength I have I borrow
Off the tide and walk sometimes almost as far
As the road by the sea. At night my breaths
Percuss the lamp like moths; by two it's good
I do not have a gun. All the visitors
So polite: they are repelled by the death
In me. Magpies racket in a single chord:
I want, I want, I want. I wish I could.

5. January

They tell me blossoms floc the iron-tendoned
Almond trees, lovely up by the Brewsters' place;
I'm not allowed out anymore. Men scrape
And caulk incrusted hulls of upturned, green
Chaloupes, just in view. Reseda waves run in,
A darkness gurgling closer, and the foam torques
Up as goddesses whom the regorge
Drowns. Read me Burnet's early Greeks, Evans
On the Mycenae. One slips from voyager
To voyeur, and now too speedily, too dark,
To absolute voyager. The *femme de ménage*
Makes linseed poultices and a sweet fig dish
I cannot taste. How strange my legs, so thin, so stark:
We ought to dance in rapture in the flesh.

6. February

The slow train to Antibes, the car to Vence;
They carried me in their arms up to the stars.
Our marmalade cat we gave away. The air
Is better here; the doctors burble confidence.
My deafness quavers in the hideous white
Of dawn: one hears the hack of young and old
Throughout the building hammer the blue walls,
And from the young girl, next door to the right,
Mama, Mama, je souffre tant. Can one
Remember pain only, and none of the joy?
This disintegrating spirit, the tangled sound
Of it, wearies me. Arms spindled down to bone,
Oar shafts: let me dip them to sweet deep now,
Row past the last red caterwauling buoy.

7. March 1st

Peacocks, red sun, and the sputtering train,
A game of noughts-and-crosses. The taxi man
Had to hand me up the veranda. The sea can
Just be seen, marcelled and dark—mine by mortmain,
Mine by the near night. Gray smudges, dreadnaughts
Steam on the horizon. Yes, the villa's nice,
And the English nurse from Nice will suffice
Until we find a proper place. I ought
To do letters now, write properly. Mark
Talks of coming down again this fall.
The rooms brown with the odor of bruised fruit.
On the red branches of my breath dark
Buds flower, the voluptuous petals
So wet, so lovely there, so deep, so blue.

74

8. March 2nd

Hold me, Marie, do not let me die.
If I could only sweat I would be well,
Be better. The flocky, ashen air stalls
At my tongue and won't descend. The spies
Of oblivion—the *bleu de prusse* sky,
Shadow-greaved olive trees—mob the glass. Dip
The sponge in water and wet my lips.
Words hover in the room, not yours or mine.
I see—can't you—me laid on the table there,
My feet and beard, escaping the white sheet,
Pointed at the stars. My lungs already bloom
With iris roots where the lower terrace shears
Down to orange groves. Wind my watch. When you
See me thus, you will have never known me.

Neither Have We Only Heard and Never Seen

Sext had rung and we were in the fields—
St. Eustace's Day (that night, the hunter's moon)—
Holy-dabbies, scaddings of peas for our meal,
Our legs pocked red with chiggers—but glad
Of the foison we'd taken in, we harrowed
For the winter barley. Shades of clouds scudded
Over rows, and then a greater darkness hung on me.
I thought the moon had swallowed up the sun,
Until I turned and saw the wonder winging down,
And I stood still, astonished as Lot's wife.

A treble row of teeth raged on each jaw
Like wild swine's—red dewlaps like a beard,
And gross thick hair that bristled from his neck.
His belly malachite and beautiful;
The rest, all set in scales, was black as pitch.
A trumpet from his throat let slip my arms.
I struck him with my spade; the monster fell.
Word spread, and two days later, with the smell,
Came doctors and a Florentine from Francis
To take the beast's remains to Avignon.

I don't know if the dragon meant my doom or no,
But the abbé from Toulouse tells me
Megasthenes writes of such flying worms
And says they do not hurt by day—it is
At night their urine rots away all mortal things—

And Aristotle affirms they eat
Lettuce to keep their health. Our barley fields
Were flanked by greens. The winter crop lags;
The laden skies are bright with signs and wonders.
For the bone I kept I've made a reliquary.

The Jew of Syria

The pomegranates bob; the tree's dry leaves
are timbrels, a music that insinuates
alleys tapering off the docks at Tartus,
nine-days' landfall, gods and winds being kind.
From this lesser shade in the shade
of the synagogue, the lingering
columns of Artemis' temple
waver in the Ephesian heat like reeds
above red drifted dust and pebbled marble.

I think of the sailors' astonished eyes
when they landed in Mandrakion
to bring us east to where we could unload
our thousand pieces of bronze Helios
salvaged from the snake-infested shores. They
claimed that as they rowed toward the harbor
the shoreline seemed to breathe and, mutable,
drew itself away from them, then turned
and rushed headlong in a limestone wave,
then sighed and dropped itself into the sea,
and all they saw was uninflected blue. A sound
of shawms came up through the boards.
They looked again; there was Rhodes.

I hear already the babble greeting us
at Tartus. I hear the camels' brown harrumphs,
nine hundred head on the docks, and bandaged
to their humps the piecemeal marvel—

see them moving across the sliding sands
toward Aleppo where I'll sell for scrap
what mounted seventy cubits into heaven
before a nervous earth recalled it down, stood,
a sun god shielding his eyes from the sun,
as I shield mine from the desert's starker one,
and dream of Aleppo, which once itself
had wonders, but which I haven't seen in years.

Biblios

(John Tzetzes to His Scribe in Byzantium, 1156)

My sweet Anselm, the inn is barbarous,
   barely yielding the spare lamp and a board,
but nothing of silence or solitude,
   nor refuge from the stench I need to write
you properly; but let this do. Repairs,
   they say, will keep us dry in Smyrna half
the week. The food's unspeakable. The smell
   of olive oil in your hair, you slouched
to your text of Simonides; the thought
   of it will fumigate these rooms. I want
no sleep, no dreams to purge the one I dreamt
   last night, as our ship pitched down the coast.

It was, at first, the same one I recounted
   in my letter you transcribed to Manuel
Comnenus, our radiant emperor.
   A horde of fleas besieged me endlessly,
their number vaster than the infantries
   that Xerxes led across the Hellespont,
and as before, they dissipated when
   I thought I felt the dawn's approach. I saw
again an artisan, squatting beside
   a perfume shop, hands clay-grayed, eyes lidless,
kohled by flies, and Dexippus of Athens'
   Scythian history open in his lap.

Binding threads dangled, and the parchment leaves
   were browned and curled as if by flames; still I
could see (at once I stood in front of him,
   behind, and hung above his bent shoulder

as though I were a crush of frankincense
    escaped the amber vials of the store)
the text, its rumored words lean and scrutable.
    But when I tried to read them out, my lips
were jasper and could make no sound. And here,
    Anselm, the dream continued past the first,
for as I stood there mute facing the blind,
    words lifted from the page as wasps, rewrote

themselves in a codex of air, and swarmed
    across the harbor out to sea. (I knew
I was on Samos but not how.) The book
    was vacant. The sea was still as lapis
and as hard: my feet sustained, I took to
    the blue road and trailed the sped black columns
south. The sea went water, and fathoms deep,
    my head veiled in seaweed, I darkly drowned.
Then the sea was sand; palm branches parted.
    I saw the wasps in helixes drain down
the sky and disappear between fallen
    architraves, with sienna traces

of jackal-headed gods, of a temple
    wrecked among the dunes. Palm shadow
hardened into artisan; his split palms
    bled papyrus scrolls: *I, Philaretes,*
tell you, not Roman accident, not civil
    war, not the hatred of Nitrean
monks, not the covetous god of caliph
    Omar heating Alexandria's baths

for half a year consumed a tithe of them.
    Here, below the sand: come, I will . . . and there
was a blare of salpinxes, which was wind's
    havoc in our tackle and sails: I woke.

I know they're there. I will continue on
    to Antioch and dutifully discharge
my embassies. I'm told there is a church
    outside the walls with a reliquary
in the shape of a book that holds a charred
    remnant of shelf as if it were a splinter
of the Rood. I will go to see it, then
    decide, but I think I know my mind.
Anaximenes, who thought all matter
    composed of vapors, said heat and dryness
typify rarity; I long now for
    the farther desert with its air most rare.

I send this letter (show it to no one)
    with Demetrios of Attalia,
a worthy scholar, who sails tomorrow
    for the capital. I entrust him, too,
with the last of book nineteen of my poem
    in commentary on and emending
the Onomatologos of Hesychius,
    and ask you for fair copies. In the event
of my not returning, send what is done,
    as is, to Manuel, and say the final books
are with Dexippus and the words of Thales
    among the lost, and miss me terribly.

Circe's Wand

Not silver, nothing so vulgar,
no, not gold; I leave that to the gods.
Let the one with those winged tarsi
dazzle the masses with his auric rod—
sorry, as he says, *caduceus*—and his lexicon.
And not just one, but a thousand and one,
turns turned from a hundred different woods:
the willows keening on the banks
of Styx, wandoo from the antipodes,
cedar, ash, teak, ebony, birch,
olive from Andalusian groves, yew, hemlock
saplings, basswood, rosewood, pear . . .
and others fashioned from the radii,
frail forearm bones of a hundred
running or reaching things: orangutans
of Cathay, hippogriffs, rheboks, gazelle . . .
one iron, another ivory,
one amber—a gift of Chronos, one slim
gourd whose tinnitus of dried seed
casts a supplementary spell, a viola
d'amore bow. . . . Call each
a switch, a scepter of sorts, my staff
of office, a prod, a piece of wicker
for weaving these wicker men, a fishing rod
for a fisher of men, a measuring stick
to take the measure of a man, something
to lean on, something to point with,
to put things under the wand, to set on fire.

With as much I have conducted
the truer music that was in each
of these who are pawing your feet;
they are all there, my wands, in that beryl chest.
And sometimes the wand was nothing
more than this, this one long, longing finger.
Sometimes it was nothing at all.

The Moths of Ithaka

[T]hey say, all
The yarn she spun in Ulysses' absence did but fill
Ithaca full of moths."
—*Coriolanus*

Grizzle of daybreak asurgent
above the surf: concertinas
of only dirge and, for the seven-

thousandth time, unrendering,
giving up no ghosts or prow.
Last ash unhinges from the smolder

that all night had conjured him
in vain, whose tongues of light
said *sanctuary,* cried *this way*

down the bouldered coast
to the tight-fisted sea.
Already she'll have been up

at the loom for hours,
dexterous in a still-dim room,
while the sinister suitors piss

themselves, snore where they dropped
in the halls—not unraveling, no,
but closeting the umpteenth

fractional shroud, winding new
butterfly shuttles and weaving
(muffled beams scud like footfalls)

enough to be just not enough
to make an end. More food for these souls,
moths that have filled the island

since he's gone: bee-hawks
with red-edged, transparent wings
pennon the honeysuckle

by the wood; the garden is snowed
with cabbage whites, blue-headed
foresters and early-thorns, and death's

heads hide among the potato plants.
Monarchs emboss the empty
throne in the locked treasure room;

tufts of ermine whites and magpies—
small handkerchiefs of calico—
hang on the currant bushes.

Emperors' cat's-eyes gaze,
and half-moons rise on the pale-
green lunas. She will not ask us,

she has not asked for years;
nor shall we volunteer
the familiar catalog of all

we did not see or hear.
And tonight on the sullen beach
we shall resume the watch

that will have been our lives
when the iron-tipped sun whistles
through the last ax helve of dark.

Ariel

At first I did not stay, though once he'd left
remaining would have been a kind
of going. I was spellburst, and the cleft

pine held no more terror for me. I longed
for the *terrae* (for me) *incognitae*
bright as canaries in the birdcage lines

of maps in the incunabula I'd read
over his shoulder in his cell, and never
been ordered to. And so for years I traveled,

Cathay to the newfound lands. Then, as night
fell one day in Karnak and the avenue
of sphinxes, the enthroned gods and temple

gave themselves back to the dead, I knew
I would return. His staff was broken, sunk,
and with it real power. But in the ruined

study were his robes, mildewed, salt- and ink-
stained. I find that they're enough to conjure
with, in a domestic way. Small banquet

tables are my specialty: celadon ware,
bronze cups and silver basins from the East,
aquamanilia, and tapestried chairs.

Since I've come back, the other spirits keep
pretty much to themselves. The foul-mouthed
one is gone, picked up by a merchant fleet;

I hear he's in Marseilles and has a wife.
Yesterday I magicked up a horse
for the old horsepond. If *you* were this far south

one day, you'd think that nothing was amiss.
Even my daily lesson—*uno, due, tre*—
in your ears would only be the hum of bees.

VI

Transit

Black goats dip to the mugwort
Sprawled on the balk, the ripe rice sibilant,
A chessboard of green snakes:

Foreground and backdrop castling, words girt
In otherwheres. Move on and dwell in descant,
this woodwind pulling up and raising stakes.

Yi Dal at Haein-sa

The mountain temple's dusted by white clouds,
but the monk doesn't sweep them away.
They drift like martyred *kisaeng* in their shrouds,

lingering under the eaves, the high-browed
rocks, the pines. The bell's slow toll doesn't say
the mountain temple's dusted by white clouds,

and still pilgrims climb from the valley, bowed
beneath their backpacks and the world; they sway
and sing like martyred *kisaeng* in their shrouds

before the Kings of Heaven's gate. They crowd
the Hall of Judgment, and as they pray,
the mountain temple's dusted by white clouds

of incense and their breath condensed. The proud
cranes who stalked the yard could no longer stay,
fled south like martyred *kisaeng* in their shrouds.

Snow, when it comes, will bleed up from the plowed
ground, and days will be shadows of other days.
The mountain temple's dusted by white clouds.
They move like martyred *kisaeng* in their shrouds.

Marginalia

I. Overlooking the Nam River
The June rains are gone and the river's vocal,
      fat, tea-brown with runoff from the fields,
And smells lightly of shit. On the steps
      down the bank, three girls play *ka-i, ba-i, bo,*
A siege of heron lifting at their advance,
      settling by a grove of black bamboo.

This much is taken in from the pavilion,
      while you read in the sutra of the miracles
Of Kannon, how you're told to imagine yourself
      on a mountaintop and someone pushes you—
Only think then of the power of the perceiver of sounds,
      and you will hang in midair like the sun.

II. On a Painting by Yi Kyong-Yun
Old gods of these high mountains appear
      as men with dragons' pale jade heads;
Use a fish to beg their intercession.
      What is despair? Reportage and landscape.
The silence of ink is the early moon
      above the rocks; a scholar fingers

His komun-go's strings. He is sick of this:
      pines and incense coiling into ether,
Ardor of paper, rain thick on the mountain
      always and never coming, what has been
Passed over. The brazier's lit;
      a boy sets teacups by the book of songs:

Past the scent of ink and heaven of sounding light
*   are trout in the morning, brown and scrutable.*
Drink the water from a glass set at night
*   outside your window to catch moonlight*
On the fifteenth of the month. Then what we cannot
*   speak about is all we can speak about.*

III. At Yulgok-sa

Built in the fifth year of Queen Chindok
            by the monk Wonhyo-taesa.
Among his legends are that he was born
            under a chestnut tree and that when he died
His pulverized remains were made into
            a lifelike image and kept closed

In Punhwang monastery, where it casts
            no shadow. Barbed pines prickle
down the mountain to the half-dry river
            and the rice fields' emerald jalousies.
You return here time and again: green tea
            in the Black House, the house of unknowing,

And instruction in a language you barely
            understand about the country
Of no language, the being of no being.
            So long exiled from yourself, your self
An elsewhere rumored but unseen: do you
            find here a strangeness fit to counterweight

the leaden, strange familiar haunting you, shade,
   a forgetting, distance deep enough for home.
O Moon, go west and tell Amitabha
   that one who longs for his pure land prays now—
How can our vows be met if this sad flesh
   remains here unannihilated still?

Sa: A Word for Temple, Sand, Four, or Death

The temple's scalloped steps cup puddles banded
In saffron, the sky stained yellow still with Gobi sands.
Cloud shadows scud crabwise where the birches stand

Haloed like four bodhisattvas of infinite light
Or mercy. Too far from here a small, hard night
Occults my mother's breast and will know no flight.

At Son-sa

You happen on it—this was not planned—
enveloped in the foothills of Phoenix Mountain.

The stream's all boulders, summer snagged
in the cassia and pines. White herons turn

above the Judgment Hall half stripped
of its black roof tiles; cattle egrets haunt

the flush rice fields. Names weep off steles
fenced in grass. In the egg-shaped pond

an orange dragon plays catch
with his blue pearl where a plain sun

spangled feeding carp. Across the river
a ferry's bearing down. Reeds that Silla

scholars used to bind their books will wave
from the peeled-back bank as you're poled away

and rattle themselves into venetian blinds
in a room you wake in continents away

where the radiator seethes with dragon's breath
and a dozen buddhas bloom on the cold glass.

Untitled, 1949
(*A Rothko in Korea*)

Gone, the slow quintet of *ajumas,*
old women bonneted and swathed
like beekeepers, gleaning mugwort
and chrysanthemum greens from
the pitched riverbank, and boys
shin deep in the water, fishing
lines luminous with the sun
as tracks of headlamps caught
in a slow exposure of the city by night,
tulles of midges spun overhead,
sentried herons, magpies of good omen.

A plaque of sky propped on an orange
sea, a strip just visible past the rise
flush with purple cosmos. Nothing
sounds, and nothing moves:
not even the river, the deep
blue center between war ended
and just beginning, between
the green and rust August fields
grown over the bones of the forty
thousand, dense as the weft of raw canvas,
under the high exonerating yellow.

Chinju
(*After Hermann Hesse*)

The women of Chinju cradle
in their laps, with hourglass-shaped
drums, in gestures of tossed silk sleeves,
knowledge of the city's history.

The women of Chinju weep,
when they weep, like silent children,
deep and light. When they laugh,
white egrets rise from the shallow river.

The women of Chinju pray,
scarved in incense, contented,
without expectation. Not even their lips
can tell that they are lying.

The women of Chinju speak
with eyes on the road east, cell phones
like seashells cradled to their ears,
and Villa-Lobos on the radio.

The women of Chinju kiss
suddenly and deep and coming
back. All they know
of life is that it ends.

Adultery
(Above Sachon Bay)

Cuttlefish boats lit up like Christmas trees
To lure the catch where once Yi's turtle ships
Repelled Japan in the bay below. Your car stalls,

Then dies in the motel lot: a brief reprieve.
Moonlit frost like frog skin on the path: we slip,
And catch each other who are each other's fall.

Flight

A boy catches red-bellied dragonflies
near where the old monk mends a fence.
In a ditch that smells its way to the river,
two gray herons stand like plinths; blue mountains,
jilted by their tiger-mounted gods, shoulder
to shoulder, keen to the western sea.

The salt odor of the curtained sea
is thick as the swarm of dragonflies
unfurling past the monk's shoulder.
Played by the breeze, the bamboo fence
Sings of a road that coils through the mountains
and shadows a once-familiar river

that flows into another slow brown river
that leads to the town by a farther sea
where I first read of these blue mountains.
I close Kwon Kun's treatise on dragonflies.
Green twilight and darkness fence
the yard beneath the lotus-painted shoulders

of the temple rafters. My shoulder
aches, and the shadow-mantled river
aches, behind the fence
of white egrets set on the bank, for the sea.
Fireflies displace the dragonflies;
stars leak through mountains'

pines. From deep in the mountains
what could be thunder shoulders
its way into the temple. Frail as dragonflies,
prayer tickets shiver. The fluent river
translates the thunder. *See
how a path is forcing through the fence.*

*Tomorrow, the mountains will not be fences,
and the road back through the mountains
will swallow you like a winter of seas;
persimmons will fall to your hands. Shoulder
your dark wisteria walking stick. The river
you will find is a blue dragon; it flies*

*down the mountain's unguarded shoulder—
its falling scales glinting to dragonflies—
past all rivers, and falls to the elsewhere sea.*

The Bitterness of Shin-chung

The great blue spreading pine ignores the need
of autumn. Once you said you'd emulate that tree,

but deciduous, the face I loved is changed.
I felt the hurt—concentricities in a moon-

lit pond again, and more, and what I want
I want. The world decrees; we are apart.

Words adhere. A sticky, fetid green—
hebona, wormwood for the wood—I fill

the mossy ear of our old pine. Don't you
pine in the evening, looking north across

the green and whaleback tumuli, the night's
shade easing from the lotus-blossom eaves

of the summer palace bower? Courtiers
and their *kisaeng* compose responding lines—

Night and day no respite, nothing still,
We too, must we eternally grow green?–

while cups of wine slip down the waterway.
A wind sharks down Mount Sondo, acrid with

burnt leaves, catches in your needling hair,
and rasps against the bark of shins and arms.

At the Eel House

Two swift beveled cuts and the long dorsal spine
is off; twice again the thin blade rides down
for the two mauve fillets; then, for so long, pinned

to the board, the eel's black circumflex head forgets
it is not there, throbs its gills, and glares up through smoke
to where green neon fish flash on and off.

VII

Winterreise

Here nothing happens, all is pure landscape:
the road, the terraced fields, and temple eaves
in tulle and shadow past the town; the eight

Koryo tumuli that pock the hills, with sentry
pines whose evergreenness seems to mock
their double-shrouded dead; the ghost topiary

of your breath; the palisades, the cold-checked
river, calm and passionless. Here's stillness,
light, and, if you want it, remembrance, a deck

of all-white cards to tell you by. Here's elements
resolved to air and ice. Here's rest.
But it's time. You've stayed too long. You brush

the snow from one tomb's listing
wall. Your left hand plays along the stones
while your right hand tries to make out the effaced

ideographs of names and laments, and slowly,
but not too slowly, you turn. Eastward, near
the four-god-guarded gate, *moktak* and bowl

in hand, a gray-robed monk walks the cleared
road back into the city. Will you return
to where you parked and follow him? You can hear

it already, can't you, the wet tessitura
of tires on streets, the melt in assurgent
gutters? Can you see it, the tilt and curl

of refracted buildings and approaching cars
like wood shavings off the windshield's plane,
and how, appearing closer than they are,

the pale west hills and three lean suns will stay
themselves in the rear- and side-view mirrors,
and the loitering dark will be kept at bay?

Notes on Things Korean

Ajuma: literally "aunt," generally any older woman.

Amitabha: the Buddha of Infinite Light, the ruler of the Western Paradise or Pure Land.

Chindok: a queen of the Silla dynasty, r. A.D. 647–654.

Chinju: city on the Nam River in South Kyungsang Province.

Choi Young-Mi: Korean poet, b. 1961.

Chosun: dynastic period A.D. 1392–1910.

Haein-sa: a temple located in the Kaya Mountains in South Kyungsang Province.

Ka-i,ba-i,bo: the game of rock, paper, scissors.

Kannon or Kannan: Buddha of Compassion

Kaya Mountains: located in south-central South Korea.

Kisaeng: analogous to geisha; a highly educated, artistically trained, female entertainer of the Chosun dynasty.

Komun-go: a long (150 cm) six-string zither.

Koryo: dynastic period A.D. 918–1392.

Kwon Kun: a fiction.

Moktak: a hand-held wooden gong used to accompany prayer.

Mount Sondo: near Kyongju, the capital of Silla Korea, in North Kyungsang Province.

Nam River: located in South Kyungsang Province.

Sa: with place names, a temple.

Sachon: a port city south of Chinju.

Shin-chung: Silla dynasty poet, dates uncertain, a childhood friend of the then heir-apparent who is addressed in the poem.

Sijo: the dominant lyric form of Korean verse, of three lines, the lines measured by syllable count and caesura.

Silla: dynastic period A.D. 668–935 (Unified Silla), or as one of the Three Kingdoms. 57 B.C.–A.D. 668.

Son-sa: a temple in South Kyungsang Province.

Sunchon: a city in Cholla Province, west of Chinju.

Yi Dal: Chosun dynasty poet, 1539–1612.

Yi Kyong-Yun: Chosun dynasty literati painter, 1545–1611.

Yi Sun-Shin: 1545–1598, naval hero, inventor of the world's first armored ship, defeated the fleet of Hideyoshi during the Imjin War in 1592.

Yulgok-sa: a temple in South Kyungsang Province, northwest of Chinju.